CLOSE ENCOUNTERS OF THE JESUS KIND
Studies in Luke

TOGETHER IN FAITH SERIES

Learner Session Guide

Brent Christianson

AUGSBURG FORTRESS

CLOSE ENCOUNTERS OF THE JESUS KIND: STUDIES IN LUKE
Learner Session Guide

Together in Faith Series
Book of Faith Adult Bible Studies

Copyright © 2010 Augsburg Fortress. All rights reserved. Except for brief quotations in critical articles or reviews, no part of this book may be reproduced in any manner without prior written permission from the publisher. For more information, visit: www.augsburgfortress.org/copyrights or write to: Permissions, Augsburg Fortress, Box 1209, Minneapolis, MN 55440-1209.

 Book of Faith is an initiative of the
Evangelical Lutheran Church in America
God's work. Our hands.

For more information about the Book of Faith initiative, go to www.bookoffaith.org.

Scripture quotations, unless otherwise marked, are from New Revised Standard Version Bible, copyright © 1989 Division of Christian Education of the National Council of Churches of Christ in the United States of America. Used by permission. All rights reserved.

Web site addresses are provided in this resource for your use. These listings do not represent an endorsement of the sites by Augsburg Fortress, nor do we vouch for their content for the life of this resource.

ISBN: 978-0-8066-9773-4
Writer: Brent Christianson
Cover and interior design: Spunk Design Machine, spkdm.com
Typesetting: PerfecType, Nashville, TN

The paper used in this publication meets the minimum requirements of American National Standard for Information Sciences—Permanence of Paper for Printed Library Materials, ANSI Z329.48-1984.

Manufactured in the U.S.A.
14 13 12 11 10   1 2 3 4 5 6 7 8 9 10

CONTENTS

1 Jesus Is Close to Those Estranged by Grief — 5
Luke 7:11-17 (Year C—Lectionary 10)

2 Jesus Is Close to Those Estranged by Resentment — 11
Luke 7:36—8:3 (Year C—Lectionary 11)

3 Jesus Is Close to Those Estranged By Fear — 17
Luke 8:26-39 (Year C—Lectionary 12)

4 Jesus Is Close to Those Estranged by God's Distance — 23
Luke 9:51-62 (Year C—Lectionary 13)

5 Jesus Is Close to Those Seeking the Estranged — 29
Luke 10:1-11, 16-20 (Year C—Lectionary 14)

6 Jesus Is Close to Those Learning from the Estranged — 35
Luke 10:25-37 (Year C—Lectionary 15)

SESSION ONE

Luke 7:11-17

Learner Session Guide

Focus Statement
Death takes many forms, but God in Christ restores us to live joyfully and hopefully in communion with God, creation, and the human family.

Key Verse
The dead man sat up and began to speak, and Jesus gave him to his mother.
Luke 7:15

Jesus Is Close to Those Estranged by Grief

 Focus Image

A very fresh grave. © Javier Kohen. Used under Creative Commons 3.0 License.

Gather

Check-in
Take this time to connect or reconnect with the others in your group. Talk about a time when you felt you "really belonged" to a group or community. What was the community and what did belonging to it feel like?

Pray
Dear God, so often we find ourselves outside of community, lifeless, grieving our losses, and confronting death. In Christ you faced death. You returned in resurrection. Bless us with the promise of resurrection and help that promise to form our daily lives. In Jesus' name. Amen.

Focus Activity
Take time to look at and talk about the Focus Image. Share what you think might be the story behind the fresh grave. Share similar sights you have seen in person. How does looking at the picture make you feel? The picture is of something literal and "real," but are there also some symbolic meanings of the picture? What else might the picture symbolize?

SESSION ONE

Notes

Open Scripture

Read Luke 7:11-17.

- Talk about the characters in the text. Which ones can you most and least relate to?

- What emotions stand out in this text for you? Who is feeling them? Which ones make the most sense to you?

- What changes at the end of the text and what remains the same?

Join the Conversation

Historical Context

To this day in the Middle East, burial on the same day of death is the norm. In Jesus' day, burials were always outside of populated areas—cities, towns, villages. Friends of the deceased participated in the funeral, as well as official mourners who accompanied the body. Contact with a dead body made the one who touched it ritually unclean. There were no "safety nets" for the poor in Jesus' time. Both the mourners present and those who heard the story would know that a childless widow faced absolute poverty.

1. The raising of a widow's son is only found in Luke's Gospel. In this brief but significant passage, Jesus breaks a number of formal and informal rules.
- Informally speaking, what about this story might be considered to be rude or even cruel?
- Formally speaking, how do Jesus' actions compare with Leviticus 21:1-3 and Numbers 19:11?

2. Why do you think Jesus was so willing to break these social and theological rules? Compare Jesus' actions in Luke 7:11-17 with Luke 9:59-60. How does this comparison enhance our understanding of Jesus' motivations?

6   Close Encounters of the Jesus Kind Learner Guide

SESSION ONE

3. As a group, make a list of the five most significant rituals or acts that take place in the context of Christian funerals. Discuss how disruption of each would make us feel. Can you imagine Jesus interrupting those rituals or acts in some way? What might be his intention for doing so?

Literary Context

Jesus has been opening the word of God through his ministry in Galilee. In the previous chapter (Luke 6), he preaches the Sermon on the Plain, which is much like and much different from Matthew's account of the Sermon on the Mount (Matthew 5). Especially in Luke's version of the Beatitudes, the emphasis is on blessing for those who are outcast and weak and woe for those who are "insiders" and strong (Luke 6:20-26). Immediately after this sermon, Jesus heals the servant of a Roman centurion (sort of a double-outsider!), and then Jesus meets this funeral procession—outside the city, outside society, outside hope.

1. How do the events of Luke 7 fulfill Jesus' words of blessing in Luke 6:20-21?

2. Reread Luke 7:11-17 silently. Chose *no more than* five words—consecutive or standing alone—that convey the drama of this moment to you. What sorts of events have similar drama in modern times?

In the raising of the widow's son, Jesus is moved deeply by the scene. The Greek word for *compassion* used in the original text means literally to "feel in one's gut." Jesus' reaction is prompted by the widow's loss of family and support.

3. Write a list of 10 possessions and relationships you consider most important. Begin crossing them out one by one. At what point do you "feel in your gut" the pain of loss? Share your findings. How do the words *only son* (Luke 7:12) connect to the great pain described in Luke 23:44-48 and 1 John 4:9-11? What is the even greater blessing that came out of these moments?

Lutheran Context

When Lutherans speak of the law, we are not only speaking of specific words that accuse and condemn us, but also of the events of life that can trap and imprison us. The reality of death is painful, and the revelation of God's love in Christ's willingness to die on the cross shows us that in those places where the accusing voice of the law imprisons us, Christ is active.

Notes

SESSION ONE

Notes

1. Read Romans 7:21-25. As a group, develop a list of the ways the accusing voice of the law is heard in our daily life. How can this be understood as a struggle with a "body of death"?

2. Read 1 Corinthians 15:56-58. What functions as gospel both here and in our session text, giving life and freeing from sin and death?

Luther's advice is that when we read of Christ saying or doing anything in the Gospels, we should know that he is saying or doing these things to us. He touches people living the real effects of the law and brings life. As Jesus gives the man back to his mother and back into community to live life, we believe that we are freed from the accusation of the law so that we might live for our neighbor.

3. Share specific ways you have seen Christ "touch" those who were previously touched by sin, death, or the accusing voice of the law. How does 2 Corinthians 3:1-6 relate to our role in this ministry of life?

Devotional Context

As you read and listen to this story of Jesus, what are the feelings and thoughts and memories that come to you? There are many in the text—sorrow and mourning, anxiety about the future, compassion felt in the "gut," perhaps the offense of some in the crowd at Jesus' stopping the rite, the utter amazement of the witnesses of the resurrection, awe and fear and glory.

1. Look at the text and underline those feelings that speak to you most.

2. Think about the ways that death in all its dimensions has touched you and people you know. As you hear of Jesus touching the dead man, share the ways he is touching you to restore you to life. Also share the words that you believe describe this life in Christ—include physical and non-physical aspects (such as emotions and spirituality) as well as individual and community aspects.

3. Take time for meditative prayer. Don't be afraid to acknowledge where grief and death are touching you. Ask Jesus to touch you and return you to life.

SESSION ONE

Wrap-up

Be ready to look back over the work your group has done in this session.

Pray

Gracious God, in Christ, you bring us out of death and into life. Be with us in the days ahead and give us faith to hear your voice and grace to share your life. In Jesus' name. Amen.

Extending the Conversation

Homework

1. Read the next session's Bible text: Luke 7:36—8:3.

2. In our day, it is easy for most of us to think that the time for mourning is done once the funeral is over. But any of us who have lost one to death knows that isn't true. Do you know of someone who has lost a loved one to death within the last year? Renew your concern for that person. Pray for and then call this person to let him or her know of your love and concern.

3. Think of the ways God has restored you to life. Make a list and thank God for God's mercy.

4. What are ways you sense you need restoring to life and community? It might be a wounded friendship or a decrease in a favorite activity with others. Seek God's help to restore those things or relationships.

5. Reach out and touch someone with an invitation to join your Book of Faith conversation with the Gospel of Luke. It's never too late to share the word of life!

Enrichment

1. There are reasons for the kinds of mourning rituals people have. If you have access to the Internet, look up the practices of various religions and societies. Sites like www.myfunkyfuneral.com can offer some unique stories. Bring some of your findings to share with the group.

2. Look at the funeral liturgy in *Evangelical Lutheran Worship* (pp. 279-285). Why is the service structured as it is and why are elements included? You may want to speak to your pastor about this.

3. Check out www.bookoffaith.org to learn more about this Bible fluency initiative. Start a group homepage or get involved with the other social networking you can find there.

Notes

SESSION ONE

For Further Reading

The Stewardship of Life in the Kingdom of Death by Douglas John Hall (Grand Rapids: Eerdmans, 1988). Powerful and simple meditations on the ways Christians can respond to a world that has made a "covenant with death" by proclaiming God's covenant of life.

Available from augsburgfortress.org/store:

Good Grief by Granger Westberg (Minneapolis: Augsburg Books, 2004). A classic and easily read work on the necessity of facing and working through the grief we experience in the course of human life.

Grievers Ask: Answers to Questions about Death and Loss by Harold Ivan Smith (Minneapolis: Augsburg Books, 2004). Smith compiles more than 150 common questions, explores the emotions behind them, and provides clear and forthright responses.

SESSION TWO

Luke 7:36—8:3

Learner Session Guide

Focus Statement
In a world of contempt, derision, and resentment, the presence of the kingdom of God in Christ Jesus means forgiveness, love, and restoration.

Key Verse
And he said to the woman, "Your faith has saved you; go in peace." Luke 7:50

Jesus Is Close to Those Estranged by Resentment

 Focus Image

Who do you think you're talking to? © SuperStock RF / SuperStock

Gather

Check-in
Take this time to connect or reconnect with the others in your group. Be ready to share new thoughts or insights about your last session. Share also one of the homework assignments from last week that you found helpful in deepening or expanding your faith life.

Pray
God of amazing love, you have placed us into human communities and called us to love and serve each other. Dear God, we try to do that, but we know we often resent and judge others. Open us to the marvel and mystery of your reign of forgiveness. Help us to hear forgiveness, speak forgiveness, and live in love as you are love. In Jesus' name. Amen.

Focus Activity
Take time to look at the picture and then create a story around the Focus Image. Talk about what happened to lead up to the picture. What actions or words or emotions were taking place? Then discuss what you see in the picture—literally what you see and what you think is happening beneath the surface for the person you see. Then talk about what happens after the picture—create at least two possible outcomes. Were you ever in a similar situation?

- How does this song and the photo relate to the Key Verse?
- How do they relate to your life?

SESSION TWO

Notes

Open Scripture

Read Luke 7:36—8:3.

- If you could have taken a picture of one action in this text that would "tell the whole story" what would it be?

- What do the verses in chapter 8 have to do with the verses in chapter 7?

- In what ways does this text speak to the relationship between forgiveness and love?

Join the Conversation

Historical Context

At the time Luke was written, Jerusalem had been destroyed and the Jewish nation was disintegrating. The Pharisees and the followers of Jesus were two of the Jewish groups that survived. Luke mentioned Pharisees as a way of preparing for a confrontation, the likes of which the faithful of his time often had with other Jews. Although often cast as villains, Pharisees were a people in first-century Judaism who deeply loved God. They desired, above all things, to be faithful to God's directives. They also desired to listen and learn from others who were faithful to God.

1. In what ways does Luke 7:36-50 support the Pharisee's desire to be faithful and learn from Jesus?

2. To invite a person to dine, at that time, was to show hospitality and honor. Table fellowship was a sign of trust and openness. What other forms of hospitality are found in today's session text?

3. For all people who seek to be faithful—not only for Pharisees—there often is a tendency to watch out for those who are not faithful and thus might corrupt the seeker. A woman who was a sinner would be such a person. A rabbi who seemed not to recognize just such a

SESSION TWO

sinner would be another, let alone a rabbi who allowed women to be a part of his congregation and accepted their support would also challenge a system of religious self-reliance and male predominance.

- Luke doesn't tell us, but what do you think was the nature of the woman's sin? Do you think the particular sin was important or just that fact that she was known, somehow, to be disreputable?
- What kinds of people make us uncomfortable when they are around us? How does knowing this about ourselves help us to understand the thoughts of the Pharisee in Luke 7:39?

Literary Context

There are three types of literature in this text. First, there is the account of the meal at the Pharisee's house. Then, there is the parable of the two debtors. Finally, the first verses of chapter 8 are transitional verses that provide a summary of Jesus' ministry and his companions.

1. The parable in Luke 7:40-43 clarifies the encounter between Jesus, the Pharisee, and the woman. Both debtors had considerable debt—a denarius was a day's wage.

- Jesus often uses exaggeration to make a point. What kind of manager would so casually cancel a debt? Is the parable only about the money?
- What in the session text speaks to the true value of the ointment? The kind of ointment the woman was putting on Jesus' feet is mentioned once more in Luke. Read Luke 23:56 and list the reasons these two applications of ointment belong together.

2. Luke 8:1-3 helps us understand the economy of grace in the "kingdom of God." Luke's readers would understand whenever the term *kingdom* was used—the kingdom they were always hearing about was Rome. Luke even uses language that might be voiced by a representative of Rome announcing the presence of Caesar's kingdom.

- Christ, however, is announcing the presence of the "kingdom of God." What kind of news is this? What is it about the characters mentioned in this passage that supports the idea that this is the announcement of a very different kind of kingdom?
- Are there characters in modern literature, the news, sports, or entertainment of whom, when they are introduced, we already know what to expect? Share examples. Is that true of Jesus in this text? Why or why not? How about the Pharisees or the woman? Read 1 Corinthians 5:16-17, then discuss how grace has the power to alter our presuppositions and resentments.

Notes

Session 2: Luke 7:36—8:3

SESSION TWO

Notes

Lutheran Context

A well-meaning Sunday school teacher was heard to say, "We should thank Jesus we're not like those awful Pharisees!" It is precisely because we are all both sinful as Pharisees and sinful as the "woman in the city" that this text can address us as law. Will we, like the woman, acknowledge sin, or will we, like the Pharisee, try to locate it elsewhere?

1. Read Martin Luther's explanation of the Eighth Commandment from his Small Catechism. Try to explain the Pharisee's actions in the kindest way. How would you explain the woman's actions?

2. The Pharisee in Luke 7:39-43 was locating sin somewhere other than in himself. Where was he looking for sin? Why is this dangerous?

Luther noted that the kinds of "sins" that tend to draw our attention are "puppy sins." They are serious enough, but our concentration on "sins" hides our "Sin" from us. Our "Sin"—with a capital S—is the human inability to fear, love, and trust God above all things. I can be satisfied that I'm not an open thief, compared to someone else who might be. But we both share our inability to believe and act as we should.

3. After a long list of "sins" in Romans 1, Paul begins Romans 2 addressing the real issue, the issue of "Sin." What is the "capital 'S'" offense in Romans 2:1-5?

The gospel announcement is that God's reign of kindness, not our sin, is the final word. As the woman somehow encountered that reign, experienced forgiveness, and responded in love, so we can be freed from our sin and our resentment and our dismissal of others to love.

Devotional Context

A very human reality in this text is the problem of resentment. The Pharisee shows us how we can resent and look down on either those who are worse than us (the woman in the city) or those who we fear are better than us (Jesus, who wasn't the Pharisee's kind of prophet). Disdain, resentment, and finger-pointing not only break down human community, but they harm the one doing them.

1. Tell about a time in your life when you felt rejected or resented. How did that affect your feelings about yourself?

SESSION TWO

2. How can resenting or disdaining or willfully excluding someone make us weaker?

3. Discuss ways we can help each other be more accepting of others.

Wrap-up

Be ready to look back over the work your group has done in this session.

Pray

Dear Jesus, you bring God's rule of forgiveness and mercy and love into a world where rules are so often more important than people. Forgive us for turning our backs on others. Open us to the presence of your reign of kindness. Send us to love as you loved us. In your name we pray. Amen.

Extending the Conversation

Homework

1. Read the next session's Bible text: Luke 8:26-39.

2. Make a list of people you "have trouble with"—either you are excluding them or they are excluding you. Pray for each of them by name each day this week.

3. Somehow the woman in the text heard a word of God's forgiveness before she met Jesus. List the people who have helped your faith life. If they are still living, write or talk to them to say thank you. If they are no longer living, thank God for them.

4. Write a list of at least four activities you can do that will share "great" love in response for "great" forgiveness.

Enrichment

1. Watch *A Pocketful of Miracles* (MGM, 1961). Discuss the stereotypes that influence how we see others. Where is great love shown? And . . . enjoy a very sweet movie!

2. Read "The Displaced Person," a short story by Flannery O'Conner. How does the story present the effects of judging some people less important than others?

3. Look at the ELCA website (www.elca.org) and find ways the ELCA seeks to reach out to those who have been excluded from church or society.

Notes

SESSION TWO

Notes

For Further Reading

Available from www.augsburgfortress.org/store:

Jesus and Judaism by E. P. Sanders (Minneapolis: Fortress Press, 1985). Sanders is the preeminent scholar of Judaism at the time of Jesus. His description of Pharisees is especially significant for understanding their relationship to Jesus and the early church.

Judaism in the Beginning of Christianity by Jacob Neusner (Minneapolis: Fortress Press, 1984). This Jewish scholar, who has been involved in Jewish/Christian conversations, presents a very readable summary of Judaism and the school of the Pharisees in the first century.

SESSION THREE

Luke 8:26-39

Learner Session Guide

Focus Statement
Jesus meets us to free us from fear and turn us to each other.

Key Verse
"Return to your home, and declare how much God has done for you." So he went away, proclaiming throughout the city how much Jesus had done for him.
Luke 8:39

Jesus Is Close to Those Estranged by Fear

 Focus Image

When you're with me I fear . . . *less*. © Design Pics / SuperStock

Gather

Check-in
Take this time to connect or reconnect with the others in your group. Be ready to share new thoughts or insights about your last session. Also be ready to share any insights from homework or enrichment exercises.

Pray
Dear God of light and shadows, of certainty and uncertainty, of hope and fear, there is so much in this world that can frighten and make us want to run away. You, who travel with your people, be with us especially in those times to lead us from fear to wonder and from fleeing each other to living in faith and community. In Jesus' name. Amen.

Focus Activity
Share moments in your life when you felt really afraid. Share also how you were able to move from that fear.

Look at the Focus Image and discuss:
- What do you think the women are reacting to?
- If you were one of them, what would you want to have happen?
- What is helping them to "fear . . . *less*"? What would you say if you wanted to comfort them?

SESSION THREE

 Notes

Open Scripture

Read Luke 8:26-39.

> Discuss how the story of the calming of the sea relates to and prepares us for what follows in the session text.
>
> - Imagine a headline for this text as if it were a story in a newspaper.
>
> - Who is afraid in this text and who is not afraid?
>
> - How does Jesus transform "bondage" as seen in the comparison of verse 28 with verses 38-39?

Join the Conversation

Historical Context

This text continues the theme in Luke of Jesus going to those who are estranged and outcast. Hardly anyone could be more of a stranger than a man who had been familiar to the community and suddenly becomes a wild man—naked and uncontrollable and living, like a jackal, among the tombs.

1. Discuss how you might react upon encountering such a person. Who would you imagine to be the most fearful in this encounter?

2. The power of fear to affect our well-being, sometimes to the point of madness, is well documented in the Bible. Read over the following passages and discuss the cause and effects of fear in each passage.
- Deuteronomy 28:28-34
- 1 Samuel 21:10-15
- Daniel 4
- Acts 5:1-11

In Jesus' day, such behavior was often attributed to demonic possessions. We might more readily speak of mental illness. Whatever the cause might be, wouldn't we agree with the Gerasenes that to

SESSION THREE

encounter such a person could make us both fear him and fear what hidden power might lead him to such behavior?

3. How does Jesus address the situation in Luke 8:26-37? How did the fears of those on the scene change as a result? In what ways does what Jesus has to say in Luke 12:4-7 and Luke 24:36-43 help Christians to manage our fears today?

Literary Context

The broader context of this passage is the section of Luke presenting the teaching of Jesus in Galilee (Luke 3:1—9:50). His teaching is not like the valuable work of teachers in our time who are usually able to have a classroom, make lesson plans, and control the curriculum.

1. Jesus was teaching often as he traveled from one place to another in Galilee. His teaching was most often in the context of a challenge or confrontation. There are times when Jesus is threatened or challenged. Read Luke 4:23-30; Luke 5:33-39; Luke 6:1-5; and Luke 7:39-50. How does Jesus respond to attacks on himself?

2. More often Jesus exercises his power in situations that threaten someone other than himself. Read Luke 4:31-41; Luke 5:12-16; Luke 5:17-26; Luke 7:1-11; Luke 8:40-56; and Luke 9:37-43. What situations did Jesus encounter? How did he respond? In what ways is this a lesson for the church?

3. If the above passages were part of a course on discipleship, what do you think the teacher's objectives would be for the church today? Try to construct a syllabus from what you've experienced so far in this study: course title, catalog description, objectives. Is it a 101 course or graduate level? What about Jesus' methods? Does he use multimedia, for example?

Lutheran Context

Lutheran theology has striven to be honest about God's promise of grace in Christ Jesus and also to be honest about the nature of the world—neither completely depraved, as some reformation traditions stated, nor perfectible, as some might wish. One of the "marks of the church" for Luther was suffering. That is, Christian people recognize the reality of the tragic in human life—situations such as we encounter in this text and such as those we encounter in our own lives. We cannot deny or ignore these situations.

Notes

SESSION THREE

1. Who is suffering in Luke 8:26-39? After compiling a list, read 1 Peter 4:12-15. Review your list through the lens of what Peter has to say about suffering. In what ways was this suffering to God's glory or not?

2. God's word as law helps us to know that things that are fearsome and binding are not simply out there but are also part of our makeup. What in our session text reveals the gospel—God's word of liberation to our captivity to fear and alienation?

The Lutheran concept of reading scripture for its "plain sense" permits us to not spend time debating whether the Gerasene is possessed by demons or mentally ill. Something tragic is taking place. Jesus reminds us in John 10:7-10 that the power that seeks to destroy life is around, seemingly not caring what life it destroys—a family man or a herd of swine. However, our theology of the cross proclaims that God is found precisely in those places we might not expect a nice God to be found—among the outcast, among the rejected, among the frightened and the frightening.

3. Come up with some examples of "wounded healers"—people whose experience of difficulty or suffering has made them better helpers for others. Discuss how the Gerasene man is such a person. How can our sufferings and struggles send us as healers as well?

Devotional Context

The story in our text is in many ways a story about fear. The fearsome Gerasene meets Jesus, but it is the demons that fear Jesus. The swineherds ran off in fear to the villages. When the people saw the man "in his right mind," they were afraid. Jesus frightened them, and they wanted him to leave.

We know that there is much about life in this world that is not only beautiful, joyful, and delightful, but also terrifying, destructive, and fearful. Try as they might, the people could not control the power that tormented the man. But they also could not control the fear that "seized them."

1. When have you felt powerless over something that seemed to control you? Have you been able to move beyond that control?

2. When have you felt so afraid that you also were "seized" like the Gerasenes (Luke 8:37)? In contrast, what did the love of Jesus liberate the demoniac to do (Luke 8:38-39)?

SESSION THREE

3. Stories about how we have been released or rescued from something fearful are powerful and helpful. Share with another person a way you were freed from fear or from what was fearful.

Wrap-up

Be ready to look back over the work your group has done in this session.

Pray

Loving Lord, you have walked with us throughout our lives. You know when we have been happy or sad, successful or unsuccessful, healthy or ill, assured or fearful, faithful or doubtful, hopeful or despairing. Whatever our condition, you have remained faithful to your decision to love us. Help us, dear God, when fear seizes us. Help us to know your presence that defeats all our enemies. Grant us patience in trial and give us voices to proclaim to all what you have done for us. In Jesus' name. Amen.

Extending the Conversation

Homework

1. Read the next session's Bible text: Luke 9:51-62.

2. Make a list of what summons a fear response in you—these include people and situations, things that are inside of you and things that are outside of you. In your daily prayers, offer these up to God for God's care and grace.

3. Reflect on the Focus Image for this study. Does anybody in the picture remind you of someone you know? If so, contact that person this week just to check in on him or her, strengthen your relationship, and share with each other how life has been.

Enrichment

1. Read from the end of this text to Luke 9:50. Note what conflicts and challenges appear and how Jesus addresses them. A new prediction of conflict arises in these verses. What is it?

2. Discuss with others what can bind and trap people in our world today—mental illness, hunger, and homelessness are a few examples. Can you take an active role in confronting any of these? With others in your group, develop a plan to be part of God's solution. Check out the ELCA website for ideas, for example, www.elca.org/Growing-In-Faith/Ministry/Disability-Ministries/Mental-Illness.aspx.

Notes

SESSION THREE

Notes

3. Do an online search about "possession." Look for a variety of interpretations of what this might be.

For Further Reading

People of the Lie: The Hope for Healing Human Evil by M. Scott Peck (New York: Touchstone, 1998). Peck is a Christian psychiatrist who argues that "evil" ought to be a psychiatric category. He presents cases of people in various degrees of evil and argues that healing is available.

Available from augsburgfortress.org/store:

Many Forms of Madness: A Family's Struggle with Mental Illness and the Mental Health System by Rosemary Radford Ruether (Minnepolis: Fortress Press, 2010). Writing from her personal experience, the author relates the inhumane treatment throughout history of people with mental illness and calls on people to treat such sufferers with genuine care.

The Wounded Healer: Ministry in Contemporary Society by Henri Nouwen (New York: Doubleday, 1995). Nouwen writes about how the wounds we suffer can equip us to be more effective and compassionate healers.

The Real Satan: From Biblical Times to the Present by James Kallas (Minneapolis: Fortress Press, 1975). Kallas presents a balanced study of the ways in which Satan is manifest in such contemporary places and activities as drug and alcohol abuse, atheism, and in satanic worship, all the while giving assurance that Jesus Christ is victorious over all evil powers.

SESSION FOUR

Luke 9:51-62

Learner Session Guide

 **Focus Statement**

Jesus is in motion to change the world and invites us to move with him, sharing the hope of God's new day.

 **Key Verse**

When the days drew near for him to be taken up, he set his face to go to Jerusalem. Luke 9:51

Jesus Is Close to Those Estranged by God's Distance

Focus Image

You want me to go where? © Design Pics / SuperStock

Gather

Check-in

Take this time to connect or reconnect with the others in your group. Be ready to share new thoughts or insights about your last session. Share the homework activities that made a difference in your week.

Pray

God, whose new day breaks upon us in the death, resurrection, and ascension of our Savior Jesus Christ, you have called us to share the good news of your love with our world. Fill us with the confidence your grace brings so that we might live and speak so that our world might also know, trust, and love you. In the name of Jesus. Amen.

Focus Activity

Look at the Focus Image for this session. Take turns describing what you see. What do you think precedes this photo and what will follow it?

An American folk hymn has these words: "You've got to walk that lonesome valley; You've got to walk it by yourself; Ain't nobody gonna walk it for you—You've got to walk it by yourself."

Your leader will guide you in a devotional exercise. Take time to talk about the exercise. What did you see from the time the lights were off to the time all the candles were burning? Note the different sights people describe. Remember the exercise as we read about Jesus sending 70 people to invite "outsiders" into the light of God's kingdom.

SESSION FOUR

 Notes

Open Scripture

Read Luke 9:51-62.

- Who are the characters in this text? Who do you find yourself most drawn to or who do you identify with?

- Why does Jesus say, "The Son of Man has nowhere to lay his head"? (Luke 9:58)

- Do you think Jesus is being rude to the three who seem to want to follow him?

Join the Conversation

Historical Context

Jerusalem—home to the house of God on Temple Mount and the site of the Roman governor—was the center of the Jewish people, and as important as playing in the Super Bowl to a contemporary football player. It was the place to go—for holidays, for reunions, for religious rites. It was the political, geographical, and spiritual center of the Jewish cosmos.

1. Who wouldn't want to go to Jerusalem? Read Psalm 122. What does this psalm tell you about the attitude of the Jewish people in regard to Jerusalem?

After Jesus' predictions of chapter 9 (Luke 9:21-23; Luke 9:31; Luke 9:44), the hearers of Luke's time should have come to recognize what the words "taken up" in Luke 9:51 would really mean.

2. Read the passages above and then discuss what is behind Luke's statement that Jesus "set his face" to go to Jerusalem. How does Luke 13:31-35 provide a humorous and hopeful side to otherwise very serious business for the Christ?

SESSION FOUR

3. The Samaritans and Judeans were Jews who disagreed on what was important and where it was important. But the time for religious violence and vengeance was past. Now was the time to move into God's new day.

- Read Luke 9:52-55. What were the Samaritans' attitudes about a prophet bypassing them and moving on to Jerusalem? How did the disciples take to their treatment?
- Read 2 Kings 1:9-16. Why does Jesus not make the Samaritan village suffer a similar fate? What does Jesus' rebuke of James and John teach us today?

Literary Context

Luke uses geography to proclaim the expanding of the good news of God's kingdom—the new day of God's rule. Luke 9:51 marks the beginning of the movement from Galilee to Jerusalem to Caesarea to Asia Minor and Greece and, finally, to the Empire's capitol in Rome. Jesus "sets his face" to go to Jerusalem, where he will be "taken up." The language indicates the utterly serious and intentional purpose of Jesus to accomplish what he has been sent to do.

1. Read Luke 3:1-9. What are the similarities and differences between this text and today's text, in which Jesus begins to move to Jerusalem and beyond?

2. How does the writer of Acts also use this geographical device in Acts 1:6-8? Brainstorm what could be today's equivalent of being witnesses in "Jerusalem, in all Judea and Samaria, and to the ends of the earth."

Jesus' use of figurative and metaphorical language when speaking to the three potential disciples in Luke 9:57-62 helps emphasize the dedication needed by those who follow God.

3. List the three figures of speech that Jesus employs in this passage. Discuss these figures of speech both in terms of what Jesus *is* saying and what he *is not* saying.

- Verses 57-58: _____
- Verses 59-60: _____
- Verses 61-62: _____

4. Read 1 Chronicles 17:1-10. How does this use of parallel passages help you understand what Jesus says in Luke 9:58?

Notes

Session 4: Luke 9:51-62   25

SESSION FOUR

Notes

Lutheran Context

Martin Luther wrote, "This life is not godliness, but growth in godliness; not health, but healing; not being, but becoming; not rest, but exercise. We are not now what we shall be, but we are on the way; the process is not yet finished, but it has begun; this is not the goal, but it is the road; at present all does not gleam and glitter, but everything is being purified." ("A Defense and Explanation of All Articles," *Luther's Works* 32:24).

1. In what ways does this quote describe what is happening in the session text?

Only Christ can be completely obedient—he walks this road and calls us to follow. This call speaks to us as law as we see our own shortcomings and reluctance to follow. In some Christian circles, the believer is called to "make a decision for Christ" and thus become Christian. Without denigrating the value of that call, Lutherans look to God's decision to call us. This doesn't free us from deciding. Rather, it reminds us that all of life is lived in response to Christ's call to follow and proclaim. Our failure in one instance or our success in another does not determine God's love but can open us to God's gracious will.

2. According to Luke 9:57-62, following Jesus seems like a very difficult path. How does God's love in the following passages help us to put that path into perspective?
- Matthew 11:25-30
- 2 Corinthians 4:5-10
- Hebrews 12:1-4

Devotional Context

Jesus is beginning the final journey of his earthly ministry. He is traveling down a road that he knows will end at the cross, yet he moves with faith and determination. We also travel down many paths and many roads, not just in our life in the long haul, but each day.

1. Take time for silence, closing your eyes while one of your group members reads the session text again. Remain in silence for a while and imagine the scene described—the people involved, the terrain, the sounds of the earth around and underfoot. Imagine yourself in the scene as well. Where are you? What are you doing and feeling? After some silence, share what you experienced.

SESSION FOUR

2. Write down a list of the "roads" you are currently on. Then rewrite the list beginning with the words, "I am with Jesus on the road to . . ."

Wrap-up

Be ready to look back over the work your group has done in this session.

Pray

Dear Lord Jesus, we don't often respond as well as we should or could to your call to follow. We don't always make the right decisions regarding which paths to take. Yet, amazingly, you continue to call us, you continue to trust us to proclaim the kingdom, and you continue to walk with us. Forgive us our failures and give us your Spirit to grow into faith. Be with us on our roads and, at the end, gather us to yourself. Amen.

Extending the Conversation

Homework

1. Read the next session's Bible text: Luke 10:1-11, 16-20.

2. Invite participants to draw a "life map" of their journeys and to share significant elements of that map with each other. Write a "Prayer for People on the Way" for all who are on life's journey.

3. Do you know somebody who is walking a difficult path just now—illness, economic difficulties, a student facing homework, a soldier oversees, or maybe someone just a bit worn out? Contact that person to let him or her know you're thinking of and holding him or her in prayer.

4. Jesus invites one of the questioners to "proclaim the kingdom of God." Develop a list of four ways you can share the kingdom with others—both actions and words. Be especially mindful of the "Samaritans" in your life. Look for opportunities to try each of these ways and be ready to share with the members of your group.

Notes

SESSION FOUR

Enrichment

1. Using libraries or Internet searches, find a work of art that illustrates what a journey of faith might be.

2. Look through *Evangelical Lutheran Worship* for hymns you find appropriate to help the faithful in their Christian journey. Make one of those hymns part of your devotions during the week ahead.

3. Jesus speaks of the Son of Man not having a place to lay his head. Homelessness remains a problem. Do some research to find homeless shelters close to you. Contact them to find out ways you can help.

4. Using either the ELCA Yearbook or website, find where global missions are proclaiming the kingdom of God. Learn about ways that you can partner in this proclamation.

For Further Reading

Available from augsburgfortress.org/store:

Imaging the Journey: . . . of Contemplation, Meditation, Reflection, and Adventure by Mark C. Mattes and Ronald R. Darge (Minneapolis: Kirk House, 2007). This book is an invitation to meditate on the journey of faith using images from art as well as devotional meditation.

Bound and Free: A Theologian's Journey by Douglas John Hall (Minneapolis: Fortress Press, 2005). Canadian theologian Douglas John Hall reviews his life journey of responding to the call of Christ to follow.

SESSION FIVE

Luke 10:1-11, 16-20

Learner Session Guide

Focus Statement
Jesus is not alone in his mission but invites all who are called to join him in calling others with the good news of the nearness of God's kingdom.

Key Verse
Whatever house you enter, first say, "Peace to this house!" Luke 10:5

Jesus Is Close to Those Seeking the Estranged

 Focus Image

Come to the table! © SuperStock RF / SuperStock

Gather

Check-in
Take this time to connect or reconnect with the others in your group. Be ready to share new thoughts or insights about your last session. Share with each other any material from last week's homework assignments.

Pray
God of grace, you have always delighted to draw near to your creation, calling the estranged into your community of grace and empowering them to speak your invitation in your name. Thank you for loving us enough to trust us with your word of grace. Help us seek ways to seek others, that all might rejoice in your new day of peace. We ask this in Jesus' name. Amen.

Focus Activity
Your leader will guide you through a devotional exercise. Take time to talk about the exercise. What did you see from the time the lights were off to the time all the candles were burning? Note the different sights people describe. Remember the exercise as we read about Jesus sending 70 people to invite "outsiders" into the light of God's kingdom.

SESSION FIVE

 Notes

Open Scripture

Read Luke 10:1-11, 16-20.

- How do you think the 70 felt when they were first sent out on their mission? Do you think their feelings changed in the course of their mission?

- What does it mean that Satan fell from heaven like a lightning flash?

- What do you think it means to have one's name "written in heaven" and why would that be better than having the authority the 70 possessed?

Join the Conversation

Historical Context

Religious itinerants were not unusual in the time of Jesus' and neither were beggars who counted on the good will of those who wished to do something good for someone else. Jesus draws a sharp distinction between such persons and the "seventy others" of Luke 10:1-2. The 70 functioned as emissaries, "apostles"—those who are sent out. *Apostolic* doesn't mean so much who touches whose head as it means where obedient feet go in Jesus' name.

1. How does Jesus describe the "professional ethics" of those sent out in his name in Luke 10:1-11? How does the church remain "apostolic" today?

You have already been invited to dine with Jesus in Luke 7:36-50. This was one of many moments that Jesus and his disciples shared the bread of life (John 6:35-40) while breaking the bread of fellowship (Acts 2:42-47). Table fellowship remains a significant sign of community in the Middle East. The meals shared by the 70 confirmed the welcome of the good news.

2. Scan the following occasions of table fellowship in Luke. Discuss what is the same and what is different about these meals. What kind of

estrangement is being addressed in these meals? Try to agree on one word that summarizes the purpose of each.
- Luke 14:1-24 is a meal of: _____
- Luke 19:1-10 is a meal of: _____
- Luke 22:7-23 is a meal of: _____
- Luke 24:13-53 is a meal of: _____

Literary Context

The numerology of both the sum and product of the numbers 7 and 10 in the Bible can offer some fascinating insights—7 being a number of wholeness and 10 being a number that intensifies the power and perfection of any associated number.

1. Look up Genesis 10. The 70 descendents of Noah listed here summarize this early census of the world's population. How might this fit with Luke's geographic theme as it relates to the progress of the gospel?

2. Read Numbers 11:10-30. What was the purpose of these 70? Is Moses being restrictive or expansive in how the gift of prophesy is exercised here? How does Numbers 11:29 relate to the session text?

The 70 in Luke are given authority over all that challenges God's will for the good, as represented by Satan, snakes, and scorpions (Luke 10:17-20). This authority is not for the sake of showing power but joyously proclaiming the presence of heaven—God's gracious rule with God's people.

3. Read Job 1:6-12 and Job 2:1-8. What is the picture of Satan presented here? What is the image of the "heavenly court"? How does Romans 8:1, 31-39 state the reason for our joy despite the accusations and influences of evil today?

Lutheran Context

Jesus speaks of the 70 as "lambs [in] the midst of wolves." Lutheran theology understands that there is always resistance to the word. This resistance is never simply "out there," but it is always a part of each believer.

1. In what ways does the session text speak to this resistance? How does Luther's description of Christians—that we are at the same time justified and sinful—speak to dilemmas within ourselves when it comes to being sent out as "laborers into his harvest"?

SESSION FIVE

2. Read Revelation 21:22-27. This is a text of promise written to people who were being persecuted for their faith. In what ways does this text expand our understanding of the sending of the 70 and the mission of the church today?

The word of grace doesn't proceed from either believers or the church because of our perfection, but rather because of God's grace. Jesus tells the 70 not to rejoice over their deeds of power, as significant as these were, but because their "names are written in heaven." Our joy doesn't come from how important, strong, or significant we might be, but it comes from the reality of God's choice to be present in our lives. Neither is our significance diminished if we are not "important" or strong or rich. The "drawing near of the kingdom of God" in Christ makes us one with Christ and the saints of all time.

3. Luther revolutionized the way Christian people looked at themselves when he spoke of vocation—our "calling" consisting not in being clergy or monks but in doing our faithful duties and thus witnessing to God. The reformer is widely attributed to have said, "A Christian cobbler makes good shoes, not inferior shoes with crosses on them." How does this saying relate to Luke 10:3? In what ways does 1 Corinthians 1:18-31 provide you the confidence to "go on your way"?

Devotional Context

The spiritual "There Is a Balm in Gilead" has these words: "If you cannot preach like Peter, if you cannot pray like Paul, you can tell the love of Jesus and say he died for all" (*ELW* 614). You are participating in this study because at some points in your life someone told you about Jesus. Think about parents, Sunday school teachers, friends, strangers, or others who have in some way opened you to Jesus.

1. Imagine a dinner table at which all who have had an impact on your faith life are sitting and enjoying a happy meal. Who is there? What is the conversation about? Is there anyone not there who should be?

We all have been called to share the good news of the nearness of God's kingdom. We don't all do that alike, but we all do that with the gifts we have. It is good to remember with thanksgiving those who have led us to faith and to remember with hope those with whom we share God's good news.

SESSION FIVE

2. Read Acts 8:25-38. What opportunities have you had to speak a word of grace and invitation to others? How do you feel about their response?

3. Looking at the Focus Image again, make lists of how such a gathering is like Holy Communion and how it is not. In what ways can your church's celebration of the Lord's Supper be more like the "heavenly banquet" of Luke 14:7-14?

Wrap-up

Be ready to look back over the work your group has done in this session.

Pray

Dear God, your reign and its new day of grace is always near. We thank you for all you have called to be a part of the community of the church. We thank you for making us a part of that community. Open us to your invitation to go and prepare others to receive your new day. Give us love and grace and hope in our daily tasks. In Jesus' name. Amen.

Extending the Conversation

Homework

1. Read the next session's Bible text: Luke 10:25-37.

2. Prepare a meal (or host a potluck) for people in your group; invite them to your house and enjoy table fellowship.

3. Make a list of people who have helped shape your faith life. For those who are alive, find them and send them a thank-you note. Pray a prayer of thanksgiving for those no longer alive.

4. Tell one person about Jesus this week. Share with others in your group how that felt for you.

Notes

SESSION FIVE

Notes

Enrichment

1. Watch the movie *Babette's Feast* (Word Films, 1988). This is a moving story of the power of love and fellowship to invigorate faith and restore human community.

2. Staying with the foreign movie theme, watch *Jésus of Montréal* (Orion Classics, 1990) for a representation of how "telling the story" can bring Jesus into the life of the teller.

3. Dig into biblical numerology. One interesting online overview can be found at www.biblestudy.org/bibleref/meaning-of-numbers-in-bible/1.html. Just beware—while it's fascinating stuff, some people take numerology too far.

4. Read the Acts of the Apostles, underlining each instance of someone sharing the news of the kingdom.

For Further Reading

Available from augsburgfortress.org/store:

The Evangelizing Church: A Lutheran Contribution, ed. Richard H. Bliese and Craig Van Gelder (Minneapolis: Augsburg Fortress, 2005). This is both a historical review of Lutheran evangelism and a guide to congregations seeking to evangelize in the 21st-century world.

Listen! God Is Calling: Luther Speaks of Vocation, Faith, and Work by D. Michael Bennethum, (Minneapolis: Augsburg Fortress, 2003). This book centers around Luther's advice on vocation and its application to the church today.

SESSION SIX

Luke 10:25-37

Learner Session Guide

Focus Statement
The God who seeks and saves the lost uses our own life experiences—even those of loss and alienation—to help us become more effective and loving helpers.

Key Verse
Jesus said . . . , "Go and do likewise." Luke 10:37b

Jesus Is Close to Those Learning from the Estranged

Focus Image

Surprising service from unexpected sources.

Gather

Check-in

Take this time to connect or reconnect with the others in your group. Be ready to share new thoughts or insights about your last session. Also be ready to share any insights from homework or enrichment exercises.

Pray

Compassionate God, you are with us all through our lives. You see our moments of triumph and joy as well as times of defeat and sadness. We ask you to help us rejoice in those times when joy is around us. We ask you to help us even to treasure those times of sorrow or loneliness, that we might learn tenderness and compassion for others from our own times of need. We pray this through Christ our neighbor. Amen.

Focus Activity

How would you describe the story that's behind the picture? Today's session text talks about unlikely helpers and surprising service.

- What are some examples of real life stories that would further illustrate the focus image?
- Have you ever helped or been helped by someone you considered to be an opponent. Describe the situation.

Session 6: Luke 10:25-37   35

SESSION SIX

Open Scripture

Read Luke 10:25-37.

- Which of the characters in this text do you most identify with and which can you not understand?

- Why do you think the lawyer was testing Jesus?

- Is there anything strange about the answer to the question, "Who is my neighbor?"

Join the Conversation

Historical Context

Jewish "lawyers" (Luke 10:25) at the time of Christ were considered experts in Torah—the instructions of Hebrew scripture. While it may be the case that the lawyer in the text was an opponent of Jesus, it is more likely that he simply was carrying on the standard form of honoring a teacher or rabbi—by arguing. Even as Jesus is privately addressing his disciples, the lawyer asks his question. Without hesitation Jesus answers by asking another question; again, standard rabbinical practice. The issue may not have been showing who was right and who was wrong so much as being as clear and specific as possible with what the law requires.

1. Read Matthew 12:1-8 and Mark 10:17-22 and discuss the tactics and objectives of the questioners. How do they compare with Luke 10:25-29? What seems to be the difference between Jesus and his questioners?

2. As you can see in Matthew 12:9-14 and Mark 10:23-27, Jesus often ended such question-and-answer sessions with a miracle, an illustration, or, in the case of Luke 10:30-37, a parable that drove his point home. What would you say is the central point of the parable of the good Samaritan? Write it below:

SESSION SIX

Notes

_____

_____

_____

_____

_____

_____

Historically we know that those traveling between Jerusalem and Jericho took a mountainous road that was notorious for dangerous places. Jesus' hearers would have understood the peril. Priests and Levites taking that road were probably on official business and thus could not become ritually unclean by contact with blood. A Samaritan, to Jews, was both a heretic and a low-life. Not only would a good Judean not want help from a Samaritan, but would never expect to give or receive such help.

3. How would you contrast and compare the intentions of the lawyer with that of the Samaritan? Read Luke 17:11-19. In what ways does this parallel passage contrast the letter of the law with the spirit of love (Romans 13:8-10)?

Literary Context

Whether the question from the lawyer was an antagonistic test or a genuine debate, the form of this text is that of a confrontation. A problem or obstacle presents itself, Jesus responds, and there is an outcome that answers the problem. Preceding this confrontation, Luke records Jesus thanking the Father that it isn't the wise and intelligent but the "infants" who see God's grace (Luke 10:21-22). He also privately tells the disciples that they are seeing that which prophets and kings had wanted to see but didn't (Luke 10:23-24).

1. How does this literary foreshadowing set the confrontation with a legal expert and the commendation of the Samaritan in even greater contrast?

Luke's Gospel highlights God's presence with and outreach to the alienated, the dispossessed, and the powerless. Here two "powerless" people meet each other—the man beaten and left near death and the Samaritan, away from his home, among people who despised him.

Session 6: Luke 10:25-37

SESSION SIX

Notes

2. In Luke 10:33, Jesus speaks of the Samaritan being "moved with pity (compassion)" over the man's condition. Luke uses the same Greek word in Luke 7:13 and Luke 15:20. What do these texts tell us about the kind of emotion the Samaritan showed?

3. If the situation were reversed, what, according to Jeremiah 22:1-3, should have been the attitude of the Jews toward the Samaritan?

Lutheran Context

A very important aspect of Lutheran ethics is that we do not do good works in order to get to heaven. We do good for others because they need our help and it's the right thing to do. If we help a neighbor only to get to heaven, we're using that person, not serving him or her. The lawyer's question, then, illustrates the need he had to "justify himself" even if he was only reflecting the common spirituality.

1. A core Lutheran teaching is justification by grace through faith in Christ. How does Galatians 2:15-21 speak to the idea of one being able to justify himself or herself?

Lutheran theology is not against good works! In fact, good works are taken much more seriously because they are also a way of thanking God for God's grace. God frees us from working ourselves to the bone to get to heaven so that we might have energy to help our neighbors.

2. Read Galatians 5:1, 13-15. How do freedom and service fit together? Is that how we are used to defining *freedom*?

A common form of biblical prayer in Luther's time was called *lectio divina* ("sacred reading"). It involved *lectio, meditation, oratio,* and *contemplatio* (reading, meditation, praying, and comtemplation). To this Luther added *tentatio*—trials. Luther recognized that human life could not escape trials, but Luther also believed that trials could give us greater sympathy for our neighbors. The Samaritan knew what it was like to be rejected and could reach out to others on the wayside.

3. Share trials you have experienced that have made you more sensitive to the needs of others.

SESSION SIX

Devotional Context

The lawyer's question really does touch something deep in all of us. We may not ask what we need to do in order to inherit heaven, but all people of faith also have an element of doubt to their faith. Faith without doubt isn't really faith, anyway. We may wonder whether our faith is "strong enough" or if we are active enough in helping others or in our church.

1. In what ways can we find a soul mate in the lawyer and his question?

In contrast, the Samaritan in the parable reflects God's compassion and involvement with humankind—and not just humankind but also individual people. God answers our concerns about our own worthiness by rescuing, washing, anointing, healing, and then equipping us to serve others.

2. Read Psalm 139:7-12. What does it mean for our daily lives and self-regard that we cannot go or be any place where God isn't?

3. Write a prayer honestly stating areas in your life in which you experience trial or failure. Name each one and follow it up with the phrase ". . . and there you show me mercy, dear God." Pray that prayer each day for the next week.

Wrap-up

Be ready to look back over the work your group has done in this session.

Pray

Dearest Lord, as you have shown me mercy, help me to be merciful. As you have given me grace, help me to be gracious. As you forgive me each day, help me to forgive. As you come to me and accept me, help me to accept others. As you heal me, send me into the world as a healer. As you look on me with compassion, help me to be compassionate. As you have given me all I am and have, help me to share myself with all. For Christ's sake. Amen.

Notes

SESSION SIX

Extending the Conversation

Homework

1. Look over the six lessons you have spent time with. At the end of each, write a summary statement of what you have learned. Revisit your list each week for the next month.

2. If you haven't yet, sign up for another unit of Book of Faith adult Bible studies.

3. Don't forget to keep going to www.bookoffaith.org. There you can continue the conversation and stay connected to one another and the Book of Faith initiative.

4. Do an Internet search for "good Samaritan" organizations in your community to see how you can help with their work.

Enrichment

1. Look in a local library or on the Internet for as many artistic representations of this parable as you can find. Choose one as your favorite and show it to another member of your group and discuss why you like it.

2. Read the story of Tommy Dorsey, composer of "Precious Lord." Especially note the setting in which he wrote that hymn.

3. Call a number of local congregations and organizations to ask them what the "entrance requirements" are to join their community. How do those requirements compare to what Luke has taught your group regarding the "estranged"?

For Further Reading

Available from augsburgfortress.org/store:

On Christian Liberty by Martin Luther (Minneapolis: Fortress Press, 2003). This is Luther's classic treatment of how the freedom of the gospel equips us to be servants of each other.

Opening the Book of Faith: Lutheran Insights for Bible Study by Diane L. Jacobson, Mark Allan Powell, and Stanley N. Olson (Minneapolis: Augsburg Fortress, 2008). A helpful introduction to the Book of Faith initiative, *Opening the Book of Faith* explores Lutheran perspectives on Scripture and applies these insights in practical ways.